BOMBERS

MODERN AIR POWER

BOMBERS

Jerry Scutts

WARFARE

Published by Warfare
An imprint of Books & Toys Ltd.
The Grange
Grange Yard
London SE1 3AG

Produced by
Bison Books Ltd
Kimbolton House
117A Fulham Road
London SW3 6RL

ISBN 1-85627-011-4

Printed in Hong Kong

10 9 8 7 6 5 4 3 2 1

Page 1

LEFT: The Rockwell B-1B, one element in the US bomber triad for defense in the 1990s.

RIGHT: A Vulcan B2 of No. 101 Sqn. at Waddington, 1976.

BOTTOM: A B-52G of the 416th Bomb Wing with a full external load of air-launched cruise missiles.

Pages 2-3

INSET: A Victor K 2 tanker showing the refueling probe surmounting the cockpit.

MAIN PICTURE: A preserved B-29 Superfortress maintained in flying trim in the USA.

BELOW: The 'Big Stick' of the 1950s was the Convair B-36 which never managed to get an official name.

BELOW RIGHT: One of the most elegant US jet bombers was the B-47 Stratojet seen here landing with the aid of a braking parachute.

CONTENTS

By 1945, the exacting art of dropping bombs from aircraft and actually hitting targets hard enough to destroy or substantially damage them, had advanced immeasurably since the outbreak of World War II. In 1939 few could have dreamed, as British light bombers sallied forth to face virtual slaughter at the hands of highly efficient German defenses, that six years of conflict would change the rules so dramatically. It had been said before the war that 'the bomber will always get through' and while such a statement had a degree of truth, there was little point if the target could not be hit hard. In 1945, however, when two atomic clouds mushroomed over Hiroshima and Nagasaki, it seemed that the bomber had come of age.

The bomber's potential to destroy whole urban areas with a single weapon had become the ultimate projection of military power. But to put a handful of B-29s over two Japanese cities and thereby bring an end to the most destructive war in history had required a vast technical effort on the part of the United States and her allies. The 509th Composite Group, which carried out the atomic strikes, represented the very pinnacle of a decade of invention spurred by the need to gain victory at virtually any cost.

But even as Allied assessment teams combed through the rubble of German and Japanese factories, examined records and test-flew aircraft developed by their erstwhile enemies, it became clear that a new age of military aviation had already dawned. Technically excellent as the B-29 was, there was no doubt that in the future, an aircraft of its kind would find it far harder to 'get through', irrespective of the power of its bomb load. Interceptors powered by jet engines and backed by the burgeoning science of electronics would see to that. Just around the corner was the appearance of reliable guided missiles that were first and foremost, designed to destroy bombers, either from another aircraft, or from the ground.

Relations between East and West slowly deteriorated as the euphoria of victory passed; both power blocs retreated into their respective shells and embarked on programs of national defense which exploited the new technology developed by Germany, the US, Britain, Russia and Japan. Germany's lead was irrefutable, and America and Russia in particular reaped the benefits in terms of hardware, documentation, and indeed the human brains themselves. Germany's capitulation revealed an Aladdin's cave of technical innovation and ingenuity that was staggering to behold — but applying the best of this would take some time, even with the resources of a country like the US.

In the meantime, the tools of war were turned into the plow-shares of peace, particularly in Britain. While only two nations, Britain and America, had developed the long-range heavy bomber far enough to field an effective striking force, the former was keener to scrap its heavy bombers; very rapidly RAF Bomber Command became a shadow of its former self. A similar program of destruction took place on the other side of the Atlantic, although it was the older, obsolescent types that went to the smelters. With much greater resources, the US could afford to keep a strategic bomber force in being, pending something better than the B-29. In the UK, the supreme bomber of the war, the Lancaster, was developed into the Lincoln. Behind what had come to be known as the Iron Curtain, the Russians strove to catch up with Western developments and in the mean-

CHAPTER ONE

Postwar Bombers

time, gained experience of modern bomber systems with the Tupolev Tu-4, their own version of the B-29. In fact the Superfortress was for a time the only type available to all three of the major wartime powers; Britain, too, operated it on loan during the early 1950s. While newer, potentially better designs were then in service in small numbers, the B-29 factories provided the numbers required to equip multiple squadrons — for while Nagasaki and Hiroshima had appeared to usher in the 'one bomber, one bomb' concept that instantly rendered hundreds, if not thousands of heavy bombers carrying high explosive obsolete, the horrifying side-effects of atomic bombs quickly showed them to be 'last resort' weapons.

Nations rich enough to support an air force capable of operating long-range bombers, realized that they would have to rely on conventional weapons for any military action short of all out war. In the light of suspicion and at times outright hostility between East

OPPOSITE: A trio of B-50A Superfortresses on a factory test flight.

and West the US, USSR and Britain embarked on development and modernization of their bomber forces, at the same time maintaining an element of power projection with more or less obsolescent aircraft.

Lacking the impetus of actual war, peacetime progress was at a slower pace; all three of the major powers had aircraft companies competing for lucrative military contracts and the decade after the Second World War saw one of the most far-reaching and inventive periods in aviation history. Company after company invested fortunes in new designs, many of which reached the flight-test stage. Many more ideas did not, and few concerns failed to foresee that rising costs, duplication of effort, and conflicting and changing customer requirements would result in a significant number of companies going to the wall.

If bomber development was slow in the early postwar years, the design and testing of missiles, while spectacular, rarely led to a 'wonder weapon' practical enough to deploy in any numbers. The *raison d'être* of the bomber, the bombs it dropped, advanced hardly at all. As bombers had grown in size during the war, so too did the size and weight of conventional bombs. Britain had developed the largest and most weighty aerial bombs to be actually dropped on targets, culminating in the mighty 22,000 pound Grand Slam. The 'Little Boy' Hiroshima bomb and the Nagasaki 'Fat Man' weighed 9000 pounds and 10,000 pounds respectively.

Despite their power – or 'yield' as their destructive force had become known – the two atomic bombs were otherwise conventional, free-fall bombs. Experiments had been carried out on guided bombs, and in 1945 these were the bomber weapons of the future – if they could be made effective.

Otherwise, the postwar scene saw air forces armed with bombs that were rarely larger than 4000 pounds and usually a good deal lighter. The US had not used a conventional bomb in World War II that weighed more than 4000 pounds; Britain had achieved much success with her 4000 pound, 8000 pound and 12,000 pound weapons and

TOP LEFT: The way it was. B-17F Flying Fortresses of the 8th Air Force's 390th Bomb Group from Framlingham rain incendiaries on a German target.

LEFT: Bombing up the famous Avro Lancaster 'S for Sugar' of No 467 Sqn, RAAF.

ABOVE: With the Luftwaffe all but neutralized, the RAF went back to daylight bombing in 1944. This view shows a Handley Page Halifax III over the Wanne-Eickel synthetic oil plant in the Ruhr.

had, in aircraft such as the de Havilland Mosquito, pioneered an effective new bombing method which was eventually widely used. Small numbers of small aircraft were crammed with self-protecting electronics and target aiming devices able to penetrate airborne and ground-installed defenses at high speed and cripple or destroy a target, often one that was very limited in area. The US had nothing to touch the Mosquito and Britain herself did not have a true Mosquito replacement until the advent of the English Electric Canberra of the early 1950s.

Stand-off bombs appeared during the war, but technical limitations deemed that they should be relatively large, winged devices guided by radio signals. In effect tiny aeroplanes, and thereby limited in the number that could be carried by conventional bomber aircraft, radio-controlled glider bombs were used effectively by the Germans and to a lesser extent, by the Americans. By far the most sophisticated example of such a weapon used in action was the Ruhrstahl SD 1400 X, the 'Fritz X'. A 3000 pound bomb with spoiler controls, Fritz X was a free-falling armor-piercing weapon guided to its target by radio impulse.

In the glider-bomb category, the Henschel Hs 293 was a 2870 pound mini-aircraft complete with a rocket motor, wings and a tail-plane section. It was, like the SD 1400, 'flown' into its target by the aircraft bomb aimer, who steered it by means of a joystick linked to a radio transmitter, the signals from which were picked up by a receiver in the body of the bomb. The bomb aimer followed the Hs 293 by watching a powerful flare burning in its tail.

Leaving aside what was probably the ultimate Second World War stand-off weapon, a V-1 flying bomb slung under the wing of a Heinkel He 111, the term 'bomber' continued, in the period immediately after the war, to mean an aircraft that as a 'heavy' flew straight and level as high as possible and dropped any number of free-fall high-explosive bombs with limited 'flight' characteristics. That they would reach the target depended almost solely on the skill of the bomb aimer, who used a sight which calculated the factors of wind speed, drift, aircraft altitude and height and so on, to decide the right moment to release the load. The target attacked by these means could be either a large urban conurbation or an individual factory complex, landscape feature, or mode of transportation.

A light or medium bomber, usually with two engines instead of the heavy's four, did much the same thing, although here the target was invariably smaller and the approach made at higher speed and at a lower altitude. These broad distinctions had already become blurred by the advent of the single-seat fighter bomber and became more so as military aircraft increasingly worked as dual role weapons. Usually they are capable of carrying out a range of tasks with equal effectiveness, although occasionally designations can be confusing. The most obvious example is the General Dynamics F-111. Conceived as a multi-role aircraft, this variable-geometry aircraft eventually became a very effective bomber – but the fighter designation stuck.

Other designations were introduced to ensure that aircraft which began life as conventional bombers would see service in roles rarely conceived by their designers, in fact hardly ever flying a bomber sortie as such. Then there was, and is, the US 'attack' category which has generally come to mean a bomber with that role as its primary function. It may perhaps have a gun or two for offensive or defensive use, but depending on the aircraft in question, few would confuse it with a fighter. In addition, Britain and the US utilized the 'intruder' designation during and after the war. Similar to the US attack category, the intruder was more often than not a light bomber type equipped to attack a variety of targets at night or in inclement

ABOVE: Northrop's famous 'flying wing,' a design 'rediscovered' in the B-2 bomber.

TOP RIGHT: An RB-57 modified for combat in South East Asia.

BELOW RIGHT: The General Dynamics F-111 fighter bomber has been used in recent years to project US power. RAF Upper Heyford was home to this one in April 1986.

weather. The latter qualification, shortened to 'all-weather', was also popular for a time, although it was more commonly applied to fighters. The increasing sophistication of radar and navigational systems tended to decrease the need for such embellishments to the basic role designation, although the elements have always found ways to restrict human endeavor in the air, however good the systems are.

As the first full year of peace dawned, the process of slimming down the wartime bomber fleets by the major powers saw considerable benefit to smaller nations who received relatively modern aircraft which had become surplus to requirements. In parallel, the rise in nationalism generated by the war saw a reduction in force levels by those countries which had policed vast empires (in various forms) before the conflict. Nations which had previously maintained very small air arms now had the chance to build up their inventories of military aircraft out of all recognition. But only in a few cases did Britain, America or Russia supply other nations with heavy bombers equipped for that purpose. Those that were sold were more usually used as transports or on maritime patrol.

At home the major powers awaited the development of the new generation of jet

bombers which would represent their national military spearhead in the future; fighters had higher priority for obvious reasons, not the least important of which was cost. In Europe, much needed to be done to rebuild air forces shattered by the years of conflict and it would be some years before industries would have the means to design and build new bombers. In the US, the old Army Air Force command structure gave way to the creation of a separate air force and all that that involved, while Russia, like her wartime allies, poured money and expertise into new design and production.

America, more than any other nation, determined that the new United States Air Force would have a strong strategic bomber force based on the lessons learned in the recent world war. Britain and the USSR already had such forces in being and these were to be maintained for the foreseeable future. While existing types soldiered on for the time being, jet test-flying went ahead in company with newer variations on the reliable piston-engined theme.

From all the engineering manhours and test flights that were conducted in the half decade to 1950, only a handful of new bomber types won production contracts and went on to equip operational squadrons. Others, intended purely as research vehicles, pushed forward the boundaries of manned flight and led indirectly to improved machines for military and civilian duties. The prime example of a number of companies and military agencies collaborating within a spirit of healthy rivalry was the intensive effort to fly safely above Mach One, the speed of sound. This and other scientific efforts pushed at the edges of the limits of man's ability to fly conventional aircraft within the confines of the earth's atmosphere and pointed the way to space travel. More immediately the increased knowledge was invested in improved, safer and tougher military aircraft which would ensure that the major powers could enjoy an element of national security. It resulted in an East-West arms race that maintained a balance of power which, while not very comforting, was a far more acceptable way to exist than in a world poisoned by even restrained use of atomic and later, nuclear weapons. The bomber aircraft was, at first, both the cause and the cure of the threat.

As the results of German wartime research were analyzed, it became clear that a number of Allied designs on the drawing board, even as B-17s, B-24s and B-29s were continuing their operational missions, would not represent very great technical advances unless they incorporated jet powerplants, swept or delta wings, and all but dispensed with traditional defensive armament in favor of stand-off weapons. All these features and more had been tested by the Germans who had speeded up the aeronautical development process by at least half a decade, perhaps more.

It was, however, impractical to redesign the whole of the next generation of bombers which were in various stages of development as the war ended, and a number of conventional aircraft which were little more than updates of existing designs did emerge to see postwar service with the USAF. There was some understandable urgency to build and fly advanced jet designs, but this haste did have its detrimental side. In part it led to over-complexity in support systems in aircraft powered by the comparatively simple turbojet or turboprop, and intricate new weapons systems, whose servicing would have taxed a well-established air force organization, let alone a new one.

However, no test flight by any air vehicle is a waste of time in an age when the best methods have yet to be fully proven. Consequently, the US industry built and flew a great many new aeroplanes in the years 1945-50, although only a few entered regular service. Almost without exception they added to the fund of knowledge which would be incorporated into the designs that came later.

On the bomber front, the 'long reach' gradually incorporated into the four heavies of the war (by using improved engines and fuel systems married to more efficient structures) was seen to be merely a step along the way. The advent of practical in-flight refueling for large military aircraft, thereby boosting range, made the concept of the 'global bomber' nearer to reality. The idea that a US bomber force could hit targets anywhere on the globe from advance bases was one of the original requirements of the B-29, and range was seen as the primary asset of new bombers designed for postwar service.

Consolidated-Vultee Aircraft Corporation (Convair) won a USAAF contract for an ultra-long-range bomber as far back as 1941. At a time when every likelihood pointed to attacking Continental targets from US bases in order to contain further German advances in Europe, the specification was ambitious. It called for an aircraft able to carry a 10,000 pound bomb load for 5000 miles unrefueled,

with an operating ceiling of 35,000 feet. Speed was to be up to 300 mph and the maximum bomb load 72,000 pounds.

In the event, Consolidated was fully occupied with war production of Liberators and the later B-32 Dominator before much work could be done on the XB-36. The project was given some impetus by the need to strike Japanese bases and a contract for 100 examples was placed in July 1943. Convair rolled out the prototype on 8 September 1945. In the meantime, the XB-36 had undergone some design changes, most importantly the incorporation of a single fin and rudder. One of the few large aircraft to attain service anywhere in the world powered by pusher engines, the B-36 had deep, 6 foot high wing roots to enable in-flight access to the engines, which were Pratt & Whitney R-4360-25s.

CHAPTER TWO

From Superforts To Stratojets

The XB-36 flew for the first time on 8 August 1946. Further changes were incorporated but production went ahead, enabling the USAF to take delivery of its first examples the following August. Operated by Strategic Air Command, the first examples were unarmed crew trainers. Among the innovations B-36 crews would have to get used to was commuting between front and rear fuselage sections by means of an 80 foot tunnel, along which a man traveled on a wheeled cart. Overall, the B-36 was just over 162 feet long with a wing span of 230 feet.

On 8 July 1948 the B-36B, the first model considered fully capable of carrying out SAC's long-range mission, made its maiden flight. The B-36B was heavily armed: six retractable, remote-controlled turrets each contained two 20mm cannon and a further two such guns were set in nose and tail positions. Gross weight, the ever-present bugbear of aircraft designers, particularly in the military field, rose in the B model to 328,000

OPPOSITE: The B-47 Stratojet entered service in June 1950, its most revolutionary feature being the 35° swept wing permitting 606 mph at 16,300 feet.

Bright tail markings were used on 8th AF bombers for identification in the air. These G models are from the 381st Group at Ridgewell, Essex.

ABOVE: As well as seeing combat around the world, B-24 Liberators such as these early D models were used to train thousands of crews in the US.

RIGHT: 'Playing tag with typhoons' was an apt description of the work of the weather recon RB-29s of the 15th Air Force.

The B-36D entered service with the 7th Bomb Wing at Carswell Air Force Base, Texas, in June 1950 and the RB-36 was also in service by the end of that year. The aircraft had weathered intense political controversy as to its cost and went on to give safe and reliable service for almost another decade. Unofficially it was dubbed 'Peacemaker' and if any one bomber aircraft can be said to have prevented war that accolade must belong to the mighty Convair product. In all its service, through a most worrying, and at times downright dangerous period of history, it never fired a shot in anger.

Chronologically, the next operational USAF bomber to fly after the B-36 was the North American B-45 Tornado. Of much more modest proportions, the B-45 had also started life during the Second World War and was, in effect, a jet-powered aircraft in a piston-engined airframe. As such it did not push the frontiers of knowledge very far forward. It did, however, provide useful experience for crews flying jet aircraft in the 'medium' category, one that proved difficult to meet successfully in World War II and which gradually lost favor with the USAF until the advent of the fast fighter bomber all but killed the need for it. Again, the B-45's most useful role was seen to be that of photographic reconnaissance, a duty on which it was to see action in Korea.

A conventional shoulder wing design, the XB-45 was powered by Allison-built General Electric J35s of 4000 pounds each, two engines being paired in a common nacelle faired under each wing. The oval-section

pounds. Although improved R-4360-41 engines were fitted, the aircraft remained somewhat underpowered. This was rectified in the B-36D, which introduced an additional two J47 turbojets in pods under each wing. These engines boosted the service ceiling to 45,000 feet and the speed to 435 mph; bomb load capacity was now 84,000 pounds in two 42,000 pound bay loads.

An impressive aircraft by any standards, the B-36D gave SAC an awesome weapon with a range of well over 7000 miles. It was July 1949 before the first D model (in standard form) flew, and August 1950 before the type entered SAC service. By that time the increasing requirement for photographic evidence of military developments in the Eastern bloc ensured that the B-36, which was never officially named, provided a useful platform for reconnaissance cameras. In the RB-36D, two of the four bomb bays were given over to 14 cameras rather than offensive ordnance. To operate the recon equipment, the crew was increased to 22 men compared with 15 for a bomber-configured aircraft.

BELOW: The mighty B-36 was the only US bomber to employ pusher engines. This 1949 photo shows the fuselage 'buzz number'.

fuselage accommodated a two-man crew under a fighter-type canopy, with a bombardier occupying a glazed position in the extreme nose. A fourth crew member had responsibility for the XB-45's only defensive armament consisting of twin 0.50 inch machine guns in a tail 'stinger'.

The aircraft could carry an 11-ton bomb load in two fuselage cells. Normally the load consisted of 16 x 500 pound general purpose bombs in the forward bay, with 11 x 500 pounders in the rear. Subsequent production models could carry a range of atomic/nuclear bombs specified for that weight class of air-

craft by removal of a section of the main wing spar where it passed through the bomb bay. Among the atomic bombs carried by the B-45 were the 2000 pound Mk 7 and the 3230 pound Mk 8.

Flying for the first time on 17 March 1947, the sleek XB-45 was found to have few vices. The second and subsequent aircraft were redesigned around the tail area when the first example was destroyed as a result of an engine explosion and progressive updating led to higher performance engines, better radar, a larger framed cockpit canopy and twin rather than single nosewheels. In March 1949, the 47th Bombardment Wing, Light took delivery of the first operationally-cleared B-45A models at Barksdale AFB, Louisiana. Transitioning from the B-26 Invader, the 47th's crews were very enthusiastic about the newcomer and a comprehensive training program was initiated.

Development of the Tornado extended to the B-45B and C models, production running to a total 139 examples. The USAF decided that with more modern swept-wing bombers being readied for service, high numbers of

RIGHT: A Russian medium bomber, the Il-28 was, like the B-45, based on wartime designs and saw service with most WarPac countries, including Poland.

BELOW: America's first jet bomber was the North American B-45 Tornado. Crews used to piston engines thought it was a marvelous, quiet machine. Swept wings would have improved performance.

B-45s would not be needed and production was terminated in 1950. Before the lines closed North American delivered the RB-45C, a dedicated reconnaissance model able to accommodate up to 12 cameras. Intended for dual day/night missions the RB-45C usually carried up to 25 photo-flash bombs for illumination. The standard bomb bay was retained although this model carried no tail guns.

Weight had also risen as a result of modifications, although the performance of the RB-45C remained much the same as that of the bomber version. Range was 1910 miles, with a ceiling of 45,000 feet but range was considerably increased by the provision of extra internal fuel cells to boost total capacity to 8133 gallons. Further fuel could be carried on hardpoints under each engine nacelle,

these being fitted primarily to take jettisonable 214 gallon water tanks to supply water injection to each pair of engines on takeoff.

Some three months before the outbreak of the Korean war in 1950, the first RB-45C flew and the type was in service with the 91st Strategic Reconnaissance Wing at Lockbourne AFB in Ohio by the autumn of that year. It was none too soon. When North Korea invaded the south, USAF assets in Japan were at best modest and, in terms of modern recon types, almost non-existent. It was decided to use the RB-45 in areas that were not too 'hot' as there were considerable doubts about the Tornado's relatively low performance and lack of defensive armament.

Before combat in Korea modified and adapted some Air Force thinking about the future deployment of bombers, the third of

four preproduction prototypes to fly during the late 1940s took to the air. This was the delayed update of Boeing's wartime B-29, the B-50.

Starting life as an updated Superfortress model designated B-29D, the B-50 was re-numbered early in its lifetime. The original order for 60 had been placed before the end of the war and with peace, the production rate was cut drastically from 155 examples per month, to 20. The first example flew on 25 June 1947.

Externally similar to the B-29, the B-50A featured a taller fin and rudder, and more powerful Pratt & Whitney R-4360-35 engines with prominent under-nacelle air intakes which faired back aft of the wing trailing edge. Other improvements over the B-29 included a new landing gear to absorb greater airframe weight, and hydraulic nosewheel steering. Whereas the B-29B had grossed out at 137,500 pounds, the B-50A tipped the scales at 168,408 pounds; with the B-36 weighing well over twice this figure, the B-50 (and the B-29) now came into the medium rather than heavy class.

With the relatively slow build-up of the SAC B-36 force, and the distinct possibility of budget restraints leading to production cut-backs, the B-50 became a useful interim type pending further USAF modernization, and it served alongside the B-36 for several years.

Like the B-29, the B-50 carried a useful defensive armament in remotely controlled gun turrets consisting of 12 0.5 inch machine guns and a single 20mm cannon in the tail. An additional recognition feature compared to the older Superfort was a 'teardrop' fairing for the front dorsal turret which housed four guns. Crew complement of the B-50A was eight and the aircraft was able to deliver a 20,000 pound bomb load over a range of 4650 miles.

A higher gross weight was necessary in the next production model, the B-50B grossing 170,000 pounds; all but one of the 45 examples built were adapted for in-flight refueling. The first B-50B made its maiden flight on 14 January 1949, some four months before the B-50D, and examples were in service before the end of the year.

Outwardly similar to preceding models, the B-50D was recognizable by two 700 gallon external fuel tanks. Positioned under each outer wing panel, these tanks increased range to 4900 miles and the aircraft was the

ABOVE: The B-29 evolved into the B-50 and gave sterling service through the 1950s and into the '60s. This is a B-50D.

first of the Superfortress series to introduce single-point refueling. It could also use the Air Force-favored flying boom method of aerial refueling, with earlier models transfering fuel via the probe and drogue system.

The late 1940s and early '50s were bleak years, with every sign that the Cold War would turn hot. Events such as the Russian blockade of Berlin did nothing to alleviate the suspicion between East and West and in the USA, military forces were poised for the war that always seemed to be about to happen. There was little doubt that SAC's bombers would be needed if war did break out and, to meet any eventuality, the production of B-50s for SAC was stepped up. Progressive orders brought the number of B-50Ds to 222.

The all-important strategic reconnais-

sance task was also vested in part of the B-50 fleet when most of the B-50Bs were converted to RB-50s. These machines had stations for nine cameras, weather recording instruments and provision in the D model for underwing fuel tanks.

The last – and certainly the most important – of the new bomber quartet flown in the US before the end of the 1940s was the B-47 Stratojet. It was the bomber SAC chiefs had wanted to display as evidence that the USAF was equipped with the very latest hardware and had finally passed from the piston-engined era. Those with a sense of history could be excused any impatience over the time it took to get a swept-wing jet bomber into service, for the idea was first mooted in 1943.

From beginnings that looked like a jet-powered B-29, the project progressed through the availability of German research and significant changes, including substitution of the straight wing for one that had full 35 degree sweepback. The Air Force ordered two prototypes of the Boeing Model 450 in May 1946 under the designation XB-47. Construction proceeded rapidly and on 17 December 1947 the first example flew from Boeing Field, Seattle.

Boeing seated the three-man crew in tandem under an elongated cockpit canopy, the slim, oval section fuselage of the new bomber being given over almost entirely to fuel tanks and ordnance load. A thin, laminar flow shoulder wing supported six J47 turbojets, two in paired pods inboard and one way outboard, almost on the wing tip. The wing took on a characteristic droop when the aircraft was at rest, although not to the extent that the B-47 needed outrigger support wheels, as did the larger, similarly configured B-52. Allison J35 engines powered the prototype but the second and all subsequent examples used the J47 which originally gave 5000 pounds of thrust. This output was progressively increased by another 1000 pounds during the development of the aircraft into improved models; J47 engines were also installed in the XB-47 prior to Air Force acceptance tests. A small production contract for 10 aircraft was placed in September 1948, and the B-47 became the first type to become a 'Weapons System' under new USAF procurement procedures.

Each B-47A had a gross weight of 160,000 pounds; the batch was utilized by the Air Force as non-operational crew trainers and all retained features of the prototype, including a long bomb bay and bombardier's station in the extreme nose. At the other end of the fuselage were two 12.7mm machine guns in a remote-controlled barbette.

Routine testing had inevitably shown a need for structural modifications and the first major combat-ready model, the B-47B, was heavier than the 'A' model by some 4000 pounds. The first 'B' model was flown on 26 April 1951. Provision had been made for two 1500 gallon fuel tanks between the engine nacelles and the B-47B could be air refueled by Boeing's own flying boom transfer system. From the start, the Stratojet was fitted with rear fuselage mounting points for 18 solid fuel rockets with which to boost take off performance. Whether or not this was an admission on Boeing's part that with only standard engines the B-47's performance could become marginal under some flight conditions, is not on record. The fact remains that some crews did believe this to be true and at high gross weights the loss of an engine could prove disasterous. The 'little bit extra' in the power department that many pilots would have liked, was not forthcoming, and while the B-47 gave good service for nearly two decades, its production run was modest at 2042. Growing enthusiasm for the B-52 in SAC's envisaged 'global' mission, probably had more than a passing effect on B-47 production.

The immediate postwar years were extremely difficult for Britain; her economy had been shattered by the voracious demands of the recent conflict, whole sections of industry were crying out for manpower on a vast scale and the national budget was spread very thinly. Apart from the lack of modern bomber aircraft to project power overseas, all RAF commands underwent an acute shortage of personnel as demobilization got underway. In addition, most of the commands quickly found themselves short of aircraft as US Lend Lease stocks were returned or destroyed under the terms of the agreement. By the summer of 1948 Bomber Command had been reduced to a frontline establishment of about 160 aircraft, all of them obsolescent and none able to reach targets behind the Iron Curtain from British bases.

The government of the day had little choice but to gamble that the unwelcome rumblings from the Soviet Union would not result in armed conflict between the major powers, certainly not for five years and preferably longer. Plans were put in hand to develop a British atomic bomb, both to lessen dependence on the US and anticipate a similar Soviet capability.

More urgently, the RAF had commitments in the Middle and Far East. Particularly worrying was Malaya, where Chinese insurgents were threatening to take over whole areas of the country. Soldiering on in Bomber Command at that time was the Lancaster, the RAF's stalwart heavy of the war, together with its stablemate the Lincoln. Little would be gained from further development of either of these types in the pure bombing role, although the Lancaster airframe proved to be remarkably adaptable, carrying over much to both the Lincoln and the later Shackleton.

The Lincoln, which first flew as an unarmed prototype from Ringway on 9 June 1944, had higher aspect ratio wings, a longer fuselage and more powerful Rolls-Royce Merlin engines than the Lancaster. Two marks were produced for a total production run of 528. The Lincoln Mk I entered service with No 57 Squadron at East Kirkby in August 1945, the unit then gearing up for overseas movement as part of Tiger Force, Bomber Command's stillborn contribution to the defeat of Japan prior to a ground invasion of the home islands.

With a maximum bomb load of 14,000 pounds, the Lincoln had a range of 1470 miles; its service ceiling was 22,000 feet. For defense, nose, dorsal and tail turrets were fitted initially with 0.50 inch machine guns, and subsequently, twin 20mm cannon in the dorsal turret. While the Lincoln was undoubtedly obsolescent before it flew, there was nothing else on the horizon and it served well enough as a stopgap until more modern bombers were available.

From June 1948, most of the squadrons then part of No 1 Group (10), and four in No 3 Group were equipped with Lincolns; the remaining eight squadrons had Lancasters. All these Lincolns were the B.2 version, with uprated Merlin 86 engines, but their overall performance was little improved over that of the Mk 1.

It was clear that any deepening of the Cold War could see the RAF at a distinct disadvantage and consequently, under the first phase of a development plan for the 1950s and '60s, Britain again turned to the US to furnish the hardware she needed.

This was provided without delay in the

CHAPTER THREE

European Development

form of 90 B-29s, enough to equip eight squadrons; supplied under the Mutual Defense Assistance Program, the B-29s became Washington B Mk 1s in RAF service. The first squadron was formed in June 1950 and by the autumn of the following year all allocated units had received aircraft.

While suffering from some lack of spares due to the US use of the B-29 in Korea, the RAF's Washingtons generally performed well and provided vital crew training and experience of modern bomber deployment for four years. This was a period when most air forces flew an intensive program of exercises, to test both their own equipment and tactics in a rapidly changing operational climate, and those of friendly air forces which would, particularly in Britain's case, become part of a gradually expanding 'European air force' under NATO agreements.

The transition from an aircraft like the Lincoln and even the more up-to-date

TOP LEFT: Few people realized how long the Shackleton would serve when it made its first flight in March 1949. Examples are still flying with RAF No 8 Squadron.

BELOW LEFT: Loaned to fill the gap between the Lincoln and the Canberra, the B-29 became the Washington in RAF service. This one served with No 115 Squadron at Marham.

Washington, to a new jet like the Canberra was a very big step for young crews, many of whom had not had the time to gain a great deal of operational experience. The Canberra brought with it a whole set of new techniques, and was as different from earlier aircraft as the Bristol Blenheim had been to biplanes. It proved to be one of the best investments in aircraft that any British government ever made.

By the time Bomber Command received its first Washingtons, the Canberra had been under test for more than a year. The prototype had made its first flight from Warton, Lancashire, on 13 May 1949 and there was a general feeling, as the program progressed, that Britain was about to repeat the wartime success of the Mosquito. Here again was the unarmed bomber, fast enough to evade the defenses of the day and agile enough to dodge contemporary fighters. And the promise was fulfilled; the Canberra went on to undertake numerous roles with equal success. There was nothing to match it on the other side of the Atlantic and arguably the biggest accolade paid to the aircraft was when the Americans – who rarely bought any military equipment not 'made in the USA' – license-built Canberras and took them into a useful combat career in Vietnam.

With the outbreak of the Korean War, Britain committed the Fleet Air Arm and numerous aircrews to second line duties, as well as giving individual pilots combat experience on exchange duties with American squadrons. Britain did not employ first line aircraft over the Korean battlefields, partly

LEFT: The Canberra variants included the T.4 and PR.9, both of which served with No 39 Sqn on Malta.

BELOW LEFT: Boeing's Wichita plant hummed around the clock, producing 1644 aircraft between 1943 and 1945.

RIGHT: The prototype Canberra, VN799, made its maiden flight on 13 May 1949.

BOTTOM RIGHT: The B-57A (middle) was similar to the British B2. For ground attack it had wing pylons for various stores including napalm (bottom).

because the Malayan Emergency seemed more important. Here, heavy bomber sorties with the old piston-engined types were used during the lengthy Operation 'Firedog', a prolonged campaign which did not end until July 1960.

The Lincoln first saw action in Malaya in March 1950 when the first of a series of squadron detachments arrived from the UK. These British machines were joined by the similarly-equipped No 1 Squadron, Royal Australian Air Force. One of three squadrons of Lincolns in the RAAF, the others being Nos 2 and 6 which constituted No 82 Wing at Amberley, Queensland, No 1 piled up an impressive record of sorties in the long anti-guerrilla war. No 1 Squadron based its Australian-built Lincoln Mk 30s at Tengah, Singapore, and flew operations from July 1950 to July 1958, during which time the unit maintained a strength of just eight aircraft. Retaining full armament, including the top turret with its twin cannon, the RAAF Lincolns are assumed to have hurt the cause of the Communist forces during their long assignment. 'Assumed' would be a word familiar to many of the aircrews involved, for very little evidence of the damage wreaked by their bombs and fusilades of gunfire was ever forthcoming.

It became standard operating procedure for each bombing raid to be followed by low level strafing runs with all available guns being brought to bear on the patch of jungle under attack. Gradually the techniques

evolved and undoubtedly became more effective, particularly when an Australian air observation post was used for close-in target assessment.

RAF Lincoln squadrons operated in a similar way to their Australian counterparts, and the two air forces occasionally joined up for a 'maximum effort' strike. The weight of fire the British machines could deliver varied according to their gunnery fit as some did not have front guns and others had had the dorsal turret removed.

Apart from the general lack of obvious results after the RAF and RAAF Lincolns had completed their target runs, the use of piston-engined bombers was not seen as a disadvantage. On the contrary, an aircraft able to fly 'low and slow' with multiple crew members able to watch for any sign of the enemy was a positive advantage; what was lacking was any means of observing the targets under the all-enveloping canopy of jungle trees. More localized flights by spotter planes helped, but in general terms this entire bombing campaign was conducted against an invisible adversary.

As 'Firedog' ground on, more modern RAF aircraft were tried out and gradually the campaign was brought to a successful conclusion as more and more terrorists surrendered. Those that were left operated only in small, isolated groups; by the mid-1950s the tide had clearly turned against the Communist cause. Canberras were introduced to combat in February 1955, when No 101

Squadron took its B.Mk 6s to the Far East.

The aircraft intended to replace the Lincoln, the Canberra B.2, entered service with No 101 Sqn at Binbrook in May 1951. High volume production of the type was initiated by three manufacturers other than English Electric, these being Avro, Short Bros and Handley Page, a total of 416 being built. Deliveries of the improved B.6 began in June 1954, although only 96 examples of this mark were completed.

The Canberra B.6 was powered by R-R Avon 109 engines, which gave 1000 pounds more thrust than the Avon 101s fitted in the B.2, bestowing better range and improved performance. The aircraft of No 101 Sqn became the first to see action – indeed they were the first jet bombers in the Far East – striking much the same sort of target, but with a more modest bomb load of 6000 pounds. Canberras could not achieve the concentrated bomb patterns possible with Lincolns, and they were really too fast to loiter over targets which were little more than map co-ordinates on a green sea of trees. The RAAF Lincolns remained to add their heavy punch to the by now limited offensive until after the last RAF Canberra unit had departed.

No 101 Sqn's Canberra detachment to Malaya lasted some four months, after which Nos 617, 12 and 9 Sqns took the duty for periods of between three and five months. No 9's stint ended in June 1956 and RAF Canberras were not again in action in the area until 1958 when No 45 Sqn reformed. Unlike the

TOP LEFT: Among the useful test programs flown by Canberras was the study of airframe icing. This spray bar on the 'tanker' 'iced up' a following aircraft.

BELOW LEFT: Early flight refueling tests included this 1951 aerial replenishment of Meteor F8s of No 245 Sqn by a modified B-29.

BELOW: Countries with large seaboards employed many bomber-type aircraft as maritime patrolers. This Neptune is from No 405 (MP) Sqn, RCAF.

conversion stakes. Their efforts were even less obviously effective than had been the bombing in Malaya and any publicity RAF operations received was often negative. Nevertheless, four squadrons, Nos 100, 61, 214 and 49, rotated to Kenya until July 1955, No 49 undertaking two such deployments.

In the 'hot and high' conditions prevailing in southern Kenya the Lincolns suffered a number of malfunctions; the base at Eastleigh was primitive and servicing facilities minimal. The bombs dropped by the Lincolns were prone to leakage, they were not always readily available, and some of the Lincolns' systems were showing signs of age. In comparison with the Malayan operation, which was highly successful, the Kenyan episode resulted in the loss of crews and aircraft.

UK-based Canberra units, No 45 was part of Far East Air Force (FEAF) and had flown fighter and fighter bomber sorties for much of the 'Firedog' campaign. The unit had a last crack at the elusive enemy with its Canberra B.2s during December 1957, and remained on hand until the end of the emergency.

When 'Firedog' ended after 12 years of air and ground operations, the Canberra was part of the small force that remained available to FEAF. No 45 Sqn's aircraft had been joined by the B.2s of No 75 Sqn RNZAF and the PR 7s of No 81 Sqn, which also operated Meteor PR 10s.

The Australian Lincoln squadron ended nearly eight years' continuous service over Malaya in July 1958. In that time it had dropped nearly 15,000 tons of bombs in 4000 sorties and had maintained a remarkably good safety record. No personnel had been lost and only two Lincolns had been written off due to accidents. On its return home, No 1 Sqn converted to Canberras, the last of the RAF front line bomber squadrons to do so. Nos 2 and 6 had flown their last Lincoln sorties in December 1953 and July 1955 respectively. Re-equipment of the bomber force did not mean the end of the Lincoln in RAAF service, as in March 1953 No 10 Maritime Reconnaissance Squadron had received its first 'long nose' Lincoln MR 31. Similar to the Mk 30 but with a 6 foot 6 inch section inserted in the forward fuselage, the MR 31 served until 1961.

While Lincoln operations were flown by the RAF until March 1963, by which time an important part of such duty was the training of V-bomber crews, Malaya was not the only area over which the aircraft saw action. In late 1953 No 49 Sqn flew a detachment to Eastleigh, Kenya to start bombing sorties against Mau Mau terrorists. Unlike 'Firedog', the strikes made by Lincolns in East Africa did little for the morale of the crews, who felt they were being left behind in the jet

While the Lincoln was flying the RAF's last piston-engined bomber sorties, its true successors in the four-engine class were entering service. The first of a trio of bombers which would constitute a modern striking force capable of carrying nuclear weapons over long ranges and give Britain a continuing stake in Cold War politics, was the Vickers Valiant. Designed to a 1948 Air Ministry specification, the Valiant prototype made its first flight on 18 May 1951.

Powered by four R-R Avon R.A.3 engines offering some 24,000 pounds of thrust, the Valiant featured a shoulder-mounted wing spanning just over 114 feet. The fuselage was 108 feet 3 inches long and surmounted by a tailplane set at about mid-point on the vertical fin/rudder surfaces. A crew of five was accommodated and the aircraft had a maximum weight of 175,000 pounds giving it, in Mk 1 form, a range of 4500 miles at a service ceiling of 54,000 feet.

On its first demonstrations the Valiant was impressive – at last RAF Bomber Command had a modern bomber worthy of the title. A second prototype flew on 11 April 1952, after the first machine was destroyed in a crash that January, and it was this aircraft that introduced the much-improved R-R R.A.14 engine of 9500 pounds thrust. Little time was lost in putting the Valiant into production, the first flying on 22 December 1953.

1952 was a momentous year for the RAF; all three of its new bombers were under test, with the Avro Vulcan prototype making its maiden flight on 30 August and the Handley

LEFT: The British V-bombers required long range refueling and these Valiants demonstrate how the job was done.

BELOW: As the first of the V-bomber trio, the Valiant entered service in 1956.

Page Victor on 24 December. Of all three, it was perhaps the Vulcan that was the most impressive in the air. A giant delta spanning just under 100 feet tip to tip, it was the first aircraft in the world to employ this wing planform at anywhere near this size. All four R-R Avon turbojets were 'buried' in the wing roots and without the need for a conventional tailplane, the Vulcan was a very clean aircraft with a respectable performance. Showing that it did not lack maneuverability despite its size, the Vickers bomber impressed many thousands of people when it was rolled during a demonstration at the 1955 Farnborough show.

The Victor, designed to meet the same general requirement as the Vulcan, showed an equally individualistic approach to the challenge of carrying heavy loads over long distances at high altitudes and high subsonic speeds. It introduced a 'crescent' wing with a straight trailing edge and gracefully curved leading edge, the whole unit being swept back. A 'T' tailplane surmounted the fin section, which was nearly 30 feet high.

Handley Page flew the second Victor prototype in September 1954 and the first production example on 1 February 1956. Each of the new bombers entered RAF service in successive years, the Valiant in 1955, the Vulcan in 1956 and the Victor in 1957. Of the trio, the Victor was by far the greatest load carrier, its capacious bays having room for up to 35,000 pounds of conventional or nuclear bombs.

Both Valiant and Vulcan could carry 21,000 pounds.

As the decade of the 1960s opened, the RAF possessed one of the most potent modern air striking forces in the Western world, spearheaded by the V Force and ably supported by Canberras. Over time, the original requirements of many aircraft, particularly the 'heavies', was to change, as indeed was the entire *raison d'être* of the RAF. After a decade of service, the Valiant was withdrawn but the Victor and Vulcan were to remain for what seemed to be the last deployment of heavy bombers as such (at least as far as the RAF was concerned), when Vulcans attacked Port Stanley during the 1982 Falklands conflict. Victors were still pitching in at that time as tankers, an increasingly familiar role for heavy aircraft in military service around the world, as the need for long-range bombers declined.

Apart from Britain, the only Western European country to support a postwar element of heavy bombers was France. Later, as her industry recovered from the vagaries of the conflict, French bomber squadrons were equipped once more with the 'home product', albeit in a different form from that of the RAF or USAF; no large size heavy jets were developed for the *Armée de l'Air*.

At the end of the Second World War as Britain ran down her stocks of obsolete heavy bombers, France became a customer for surplus equipment. Even more than the RAF,

the French had been reliant on the US to provide the equipment for a regenerated bomber strike force built primarily around the three USAAF light types, the A-20, B-25 and B-26. The French flew Halifaxes from Britain as part of RAF Bomber Command during the last years of the war and when hostilities ceased these machines went home with their French crews, US Lend Lease stocks having been returned.

The urgent need for transports rather than bombers saw the Halifaxes used more in that role until they were retired; the most important requirement for the French air force after the war was to initiate training programs and standardize a manageable number of types for basic defense duties both in France and her overseas territories. There was little need for a bomber force, other than for the kind of ground support mission that could be largely undertaken by fighters. In the reconnaissance role, the *Armée de l'Air* employed the DH Mosquito but otherwise converted all *Groupes de Bombardement* to the transport role for the time being. The pressing need to streamline and standardize on a small number of types is shown by the fact that during 1946-47, no less than 88 different types flew in French markings, only two of which were indigenous.

Equally assorted was the equipment of the French navy. Its patrol bombers included Vickers Wellingtons, Avro Lancasters and Convair PB4Y-2 Privateers, there being an additional patrol force composed of American P2V-6 and -7 Neptunes and the Grumman JRF-5 Goose.

TOP LEFT: A B2 Vulcan releasing a maximum bomb load from its capacious bay.

LEFT: The Victor was more commonly used as a tanker, despite excellent bombing capabilities.

RIGHT: A cell of 1000 pound bombs goes into a Vulcan.

BELOW RIGHT: Few service Neptunes flew in natural metal finish, this being an early example of the last major model, the P2V-7.

Soviet Russia, well able to produce reliable, tough combat aircraft tailored to her own unique operating conditions, had gained parity with the West in many aeronautical fields at the end of World War II. The injection of captured German research data spurred a vast effort to get jet bombers and fighters into service as soon as possible. Few other nations carried out so much work in the field of military aviation as the Soviets did in the late 1940s; numerous designs reached flight test stage with the result that the successors to the predominantly fighter and ground attack aircraft that had won the 'Great Patriotic War' were among the most potent in the world.

Having operated only one long-range heavy bomber, the Pe-8, during the war years, the postwar Soviet air force saw the need to police the newly acquired satellite states and her own far-flung borders with aircraft that could stay airborne for extremely long periods, deliver, if necessary, a new range of weapons, and return home to bases deep inside Russian territory. The horrors of the German occupation had gone very deep — there was little desire to risk such an invasion again through military unprepardness. The arms race that the Soviet leaders had been instrumental in creating produced its own grim momentum — once in, neither East nor West could afford to draw back.

Possession of atomic and nuclear weapons gave the Soviet Union superpower status and from small beginnings the Communist giant gained parity and in many instances, a lead, over the forces that might one day be ranged against her. Technically, the Russians were often ahead of the West and numerically, they never fell behind.

With the war at an end, the VVS had ample numbers of twin-engined modern bombers such as the Pe-2 and Tu-2 in service. Production of these and other types continued, so that most Eastern European air arms could be supplied and thereby achieve some degree of standardization. But what the Red air force now required was a bomber in the B-29 class, which then represented the peak of strategic bomber development.

Efforts to obtain B-29s under Lend Lease agreements failed and the Soviets could do little but fall back on design studies. The problem was that the manufacture of multi-engine types was outside the experience of most designers, particularly if such aircraft were to feature such contemporary items as pressurization and remotely controlled armament systems. Given time, Soviet long-range bombers would undoubtedly have appeared — but to make the quantum leap from short-range piston-engined types to far larger airframes taking power from multiple turbojet units was quite daunting. The request for allocation of B-29s under Lend Lease was to provide an ideal — if technically temporary — starting point for modern bomber production. Fortunately for the Soviets, three B-29s became available in 1944. Having begun design studies for a similar Soviet bomber, the windfall B-29s were literally taken apart panel by panel and used as patterns for a similar bomber.

The resultant Soviet version of the B-29, while externally similar to the Boeing original, was very different in virtually all respects. The facilities and experience available in Seattle or Wichita could not then be duplicated by Tupolev's design bureau. Nevertheless, the gigantic task was completed and the first Tu-4 flew on 3 July 1947. Far more than just another maiden flight,

CHAPTER FOUR

The Red Airforce

the Tu-4 represented an inestimably valuable leap forward in Soviet know-how as pertaining to large, modern airframes. From the Tu-4 stemmed a whole series of aircraft that formed the basis for modernization of the industry responsible for this class of project. Some 300 Tu-4s were in VVS service by 1950.

Although the strategic bomber had high priority in the Soviet Union, the need to re-equip ground support formations with more modern aircraft was not overlooked. A category of aircraft in which the Russians had long excelled and which were relatively easy to produce in the required high numbers, there was no shortage of new design submissions in this important category.

Apart from the maiden flight of the Il-22 in July 1947 the first postwar turbojet four-jet bomber design to fly in Europe, and the first ever in Russia, was the Il-28. Whereas the Il-22 had four separate jet pods and a high wing configuration similar to that of the

LEFT: The tail position on a Soviet Tu-95 Bear-D showing the Box Tail radar fairing and a couple of crew portraits, taken by a NATO aircraft.

ABOVE: Western fighters spend a lot of time intercepting and escorting Russian Bears out of friendly airspace. This one goes on its way after being photographed.

TOP RIGHT: The Tu-22 Blinder of which about 250 were built, was the first Soviet supersonic bomber.

BELOW RIGHT: The Il-28 was an elegant design that served for many years and was even copied by the Chinese.

Arado Ar 234C and was classed as a medium bomber with a maximum loaded weight of 52,900 pounds, the twin jet Il-28 was larger but in standard form had a loaded weight about 12,000 pounds less. Often compared with the British Canberra, the Il-28 went on to serve in at least 15 other air arms as well as the VVS and was license-built in China. It was also to see action in the markings of nearly half the nations to which it was supplied.

Chronologically the next Soviet bomber to enter service was the Tu-14, another twin-jet which although originally intended for the VVS, operated solely with the Soviet naval air arm, and only in small numbers.

Tupolev designs had begun to dominate the Soviet bomber scene, a situation that was to continue. Along with the machines that were actually brought into service with the air force and navy, the Tupolev design bureau or OKB produced the Tu-80 and Tu-85, both being excellent designs in the four engine class and the ultimate stretch of the basic Tu-4/B-29 copy. The OKB cut its jet teeth on a Rolls-Royce Nene powered Tu-2 and progressed to a more practical installation (the original had had the jet engines in an underslung fuselage pod) with two jets but it was still very much like a Tu-2.

The Tu-16, code-named Badger, under the NATO reporting system for Soviet aircraft, was another leap forward. It was the largest jet aircraft the country had produced at the time of its first flight in early 1952, and it gave the VVS its first jet intercontinental bomber. Featuring a 108 foot wing with a maximum 35 degrees sweepback at the tips, the Tu-16 was powered by two RD-3 turbojets flanking both sides of the fuselage, the wings being attached to the outside face of each nacelle. The wing was 'wet' and unbroken by bays for undercarriage stowage; the mainwheels and oleos retracted into what became

something of a Soviet design hallmark, pods protruding aft of the wing trailing edge.

In original bomber form, the Tu-16 carried a heavy defensive armament of six 23mm guns in three remote-controlled turrets, as well as a seventh weapon fired by the pilot from the right side of the nose. The bomb bay held 19,841 pounds of stores, and succeeding versions had underwing hardpoints for AS-1 anti-shipping missiles.

The Tu-16 is understood to have entered VVS service in 1954 and was, like numerous other Soviet aircraft, destined to stay in service for many years. Lacking reliable sub-variant designations, the NATO reporting system has identified at least 10 Badger variants, each modified for dual bombing, anti-shipping, ECM and tanker duties, among others.

Never averse to surprising the rest of the world with its inventiveness in the field of aeronautics, the Soviet aerospace industry has claimed many 'firsts'. Among these was the adaptation of the turboprop to military use in the mighty Tu-20. Representing the logical extension of the outstanding Tu-85 concept, without losing some family resemblance to the straight-winged original, the Bear has been around since its first flight in the autumn of 1954.

LEFT: A menacing TU-16 Badger long-range reconnaissance aircraft.

Just as the superpowers were developing new bombers for the war most people hoped would never come, conflict erupted in Korea. When North Korea invaded her neighbour across the 38th parallel of latitude on 25 June 1950, only a handful of bombers was available to Far Eastern air forces. On Guam in the Marianas was the 19th Bomb Group, the nearest US unit to the scene of action, with just 22 B-29s. As the situation worsened for the United Nations command, these aircraft were sent over North Korea to seek targets of opportunity.

In order to maintain pressure on North Korea's industrial center, SAC despatched two more B-29 groups, the 22nd and 92nd to Yokota, Japan, where FEAF established a bomber command HQ to direct operations. The 19th was very quick off the mark, flying its first mission on 27 June, one day before official US support for the South Korean cause was announced. The crews, who were briefed to fly initially to Kadena AB on Okinawa to bring Korea in range of their aircraft, were told to take with them only a few extra items, plus one flight suit, in the belief that their combat 'tour' would last about a week. It took a little longer than that – it was three years before the group returned home.

The B-29s attacked in small formations for mutual safety against air interception. In those early days the 19th Group struck airfields, troop concentrations and railway targets as part of the desperate and ill-planned offensive to stop the North Korean advance. Early in July the 22nd and 92nd Groups arrived to support what amounted to a bridgehead around the port of Pusan at the extreme southeast corner of the peninsula. All available airpower assets (including Superfortresses) were flung into the battle against enemy ground forces. Arriving individually over the battle line at 30-minute intervals the bombers were directed on to their targets by 5th AF controlers who assigned aircraft to meet a fluid situation. Such pin-point bombing was very difficult for the B-29 crews and was not what the aircraft had been designed for; after 18 July it was discontinued, pending more effective deployment.

By 5 August, with the ground situation easing, the 98th and 307th Groups had arrived and begun combat operations. SAC drew up a list of 18 strategic targets in North Korea and, in a very short time, the B-29s had taken out almost all North Korea's industry. By so doing the American crews came dangerously close to the country's border with China and they were briefed to ensure that, as far as possible, their bombs fell in the right place. This was particularly true of oil storage facilities located at Rashin, only 17 miles from China. After one abortive strike, Rashin was taken off the target list.

Others were successfully bombed. They included one of the largest oil refineries in the Far East, locomotive repair shops at Wonsan, an explosives and chemical plant at Hungnam and the source of most of the country's armaments near the capital, Pyongyang. The Superfortress campaign was without any air opposition to speak of and highly successful. FEAF Bomber Command had all five B-29 groups under its control, even though the 19th was not part of SAC; it remained a more or less independent force, and was able to run quickly down the target list and cross each one off as destroyed or badly damaged.

By September the strategic campaign was all but over – indeed when MacArthur's forces from Inchon linked up with the de-

CHAPTER FIVE

Korea

fenders of Pusan and made a headlong dash northwards, the war seemed as good as won. UN forces reoccupied Seoul on 26 September and less than a month later, American and South Korean troops were in the streets of Pyongyang. So complete did the victory seem that FEAF sent the 22nd and 92nd Groups home to the US.

But as Truman and the chiefs of staff had feared, the Chinese were not going to stand by and watch North Korea be forcibly reunified with the South. In November 1950 there came the first signs of massive troop movements along the Yalu River and the B-29 force was sent against the southern approaches to the bridges that linked Korea with Manchuria, with the objective of wrecking the rail and road system into the North. With the weather deteriorating and the Yalu beginning to freeze over, the task was hard; in addition, limited North Korean fighter opposition had begun. On 15 November, MiG-15s hit the B-29s during a raid on the

TOP LEFT: The flight deck of a B-29 showing the co-pilot's seat and the bombadier's station in the nose.

BELOW LEFT: A B-29 of the 98th Bomb Wing at Yokota, Japan being refueled for a mission over Korea.

ABOVE: B-29 mediums of the 92nd Wing over Korea.

TOP RIGHT: Recalled to duty in Korea, the B-26 Invader gave sterling service. This 3rd BW aircraft releases 500 lb bombs.

RIGHT: An RB-29 of the 90th Bomb Wing.

bridges at Sinui-ju, damaging two bombers.

The Chinese tide flooded into North Korea, forcing UN troops to retreat; in the air the UN remained in control, the enemy never committing his air force to a sustained ground attack campaign. Interceptions of UN aircraft were sporadic, despite the availability of the MiG-15. Well flown and attacking under disciplined, co-ordinated control, frequent sorties by MiG-15s could have made losses of B-29s prohibitive. As it was, the NKAF chose to press home attacks only on occasion.

The first B-29 was lost on 30 November when an aircraft of the 31st Reconnaissance Sqn, previously damaged by flak, was forced down, fortunately in South Korea. The 31st had responded to an order to move to Korea with the 22nd and 92nd in July, its RB-29s offering SAC a useful in-theater recon service for potential Korean targets.

Weather continued to curtail air operations through December and the early weeks of 1951 and, by the end of January, a battle line was established some 50 miles south of the 38th parallel. When conditions allowed, the US medium bombers maintained the pressure on enemy supply centers and lines of communication. In January 1951, they

made two incendiary attacks on Pyongyang to destroy supplies.

As the ChiCom build up continued, so more fighters were moved up to occupy airfields near the Yalu. American pilots kept to the southern side of the river, allowing the enemy to pick the time and place of his attack and hightail it back to his bases if the UN reaction got too strong. 'MiG Alley' became potentially lethal to most UN fighters and bombers, all of which, with the exception of the F-86 Sabre, were outclassed by the MiG-15.

To meet the threat, FEAF stopped forays by small numbers of bombers and reverted to the 'safety in numbers' formations that had proved so successful against fighter attack in World War II. Escorts were also provided for the B-29s, with the Sabres sweeping ahead to deal with any MiG threat as far as their limited endurance allowed. After March 1951 it was decided to switch B-29s to night attacks in the light of limited availability of Sabres for escort duty. The mediums began using 2000 pound Razon and 12,000 pound Tarzon radio-controlled bombs against targets that were hard to hit with conventional high explosives. Overcoming various problems with the special bombs – including the fact that they could not be jettisoned on 'safe'

– the crews grew increasingly proficient at taking out bridges and airfields as well as a host of other targets. Airfields required daylight formations to put down an effective bomb pattern and a number of such strikes were flown in the autumn of 1951. In October, five B-29s were lost on these missions.

The Superfortress crews tried a variety of tactics to surprise the defenses, hit the targets and minimize their own losses. The enemy countered with searchlights and AA guns as well as fighter interception. The second half of 1951 saw a determined effort by the NKAF to gain air superiority, but it failed to do so. Even so, the margin was narrow; better experience and training, plus the determination to complete the mission, were the deciding factors in the UN's favor. The MiG pilots never succeeded in stopping the air interdiction campaign against their comrades on the ground. Throughout the war, air action fluctuated: some raids would be hotly challenged, while others would be carried out almost without interference, at least by fighters. The B-29s employed radar bombing aids such as Shoran, whereby two ground stations in friendly territory transmitted beams to intersect over the target area and give the bombardiers a precise release point. These techniques increased the

BELOW LEFT: The B-26 was another stalwart bomber. First used during the Second World War, the Invader provided wide-ranging cover in Korea, and its service-life extended to napalm raids in Vietnam in the 1960s (pictured here).

BELOW: F-86 Sabres of the 52nd Wing on patrol. They protected UN bomber forces and slower jet types against interception by MiG-15s.

USAF's edge over the opposition so that the 'bomb line' could be pushed further and further north.

North Korean searchlights posed a serious problem and although some respite was gained by having B-26s attack them while the B-29s followed up to bomb from high altitude, aircraft coned by lights stood little chance. This was proved in June 1952 when two B-29s were destroyed by guns after being held by about 20 searchlights and a third aircraft barely made it home to Kimpo.

As the war and the peace talks to end it dragged on into a third year, the ChiCom effort to stop night bombing raids did not slacken. Night fighters were introduced into the formations, and these achieved a number of nocturnal air-to-air kills. Low down, Invaders were keeping up their interdiction war against the North Korean transportation system and key points of the enemy air defense net. Radar was undoubtedly the key to UN success and by the end of 1952 targets only four miles from the Yalu were being attacked. Radio countermeasures, plus the time-honored dropping of 'Window' by the bombers, also made a significant contribution. Psychological warfare had also entered the picture and B-29s dumped millions of leaflets over North Korea. A prime aim of this

paper war was to persuade a MiG pilot to defect with his aircraft so that a full evaluation could be made. In the event, even the offer of $100,000 and political asylum was not inducement enough while hostilities continued, but after the armistice, the US got its MiG.

At peak strength, the number of B-29s available for Korean combat operations was never more than 170 aircraft and more generally the strength of three groups was around 110. During the 37-month war Superforts dropped 185,000 tons of bombs in more than 22,000 sorties. On the debit side, 16 were lost to fighters and four to flak, with another 14 written off in accidents and other operational causes – a total of 34 aircraft. That made one B-29 in every 600-plus sorties, a respectable return. Gunners claimed an impressive 33 enemy fighters, including 16 MiGs shot down.

When the Korean war ended on 27 July 1953, it represented the end of an era. The piston-engined bomber was finally laid to rest as a front line type in the strategic role, although the beat of reciprocating engines would be heard over battlefields in the tactical task for many years to come.

The B-26 was used for the exacting tactical mission in Korea, the 'low and slow', work

TOP: The C-47 Skytrain saw widespread service in both Korea and Vietnam, flying every kind of sortie from gunship to psychological warfare.

ABOVE: The cramped quarters of a B-29's bombardier.

troops, the B-26s used their heavy built-in armament and useful stores load to good effect. An aircraft with a better endurance than the jet ground attack types, the Invader ranged far and wide, punching holes in enemy supply lines by day and night. Nocturnal sorties were initially helped by the fact that North Korean truck drivers habitually kept their headlights on, and by illumination with air-dropped flares released by B-29s and C-47s.

The 452nd arrived in October 1950, providing a welcome boost to the intruder force. When the Chinese attacked, the Invaders went increasingly over to night interdiction before some stabilization of the front assisted the location of enemy targets. As with the B-29 mediums, the attack squadrons tried every trick in the book, as well as some new ones, to stop the flow of supplies to the troops in the south. In general the strikes were effective and they certainly helped curtail operations in certain sectors at various times. But the Chinese had almost limitless reserves of manpower to fill craters, shore-up breaks in river crossings and simply carry supplies on their backs, and the real answer was a much larger air offensive than was ever possible in Korea. Undaunted, the USAF carried on with what resources it had.

The enemy soon learned to blacken out his night convoys and it became clear that to maintain the pressure, it would be sound practice to divide the B-26 force, enabling the crews to gain intimate knowledge of their sectors so that even at night, they would know where to look for targets. Consequently, the 3rd Wing took over western Korea and the 452nd shouldered responsibility for eastern regions. With more B-26Cs available, the bombardier became an integral member of the attack bomber crew.

Radar and blind bombing were tried with some success, as was the use of searchlights carried under the Invaders' wings, although this had the disadvantage of illuminating the carrier aircraft. On only rare occasions were the B-26s obliged to combat the enemy in the air and in a number of skirmishes a few claims were made by American crews.

By far the most successful technique for denying the enemy the cover of darkness was the 'hunter-killer' team of a flare-dropping C-47 and a pair of B-26s. Pioneered by the 731st Sqn, the deployment of an orbiting C-47 creating near-daylight conditions for the devastating Invader attack, prevented any significant night advance by ChiCom forces after May 1951. There was no doubt that enemy trains and road transport could be destroyed at night by the B-26 crews — they only needed to see them for a short period of time. That period was provided by the modified flare ships.

which rarely grabbed the headlines. A well-liked maid-of-all-work since its debut as a light attack bomber in World War II, the Invader was flown in Korea by the 3rd, 452nd, and 17th Wings, plus the independent and highly specialized 731st Bomb Squadron and the equally specialized 67th Tac Recon Wing.

From the start, the 3rd faced a whole set of problems in interdicting North Korean traffic, not least of which was shortage of aircraft. Nevertheless the Wing carried the war to the enemy and quickly piled up high mission totals against the weather, flak and the Korean terrain, hazards not necessarily in that order. In supporting friendly ground

TOP: Test flight for a production B-26 Invader.

RIGHT: An engineer surveys the tail of a B-45 Tornado, a bomber that saw limited service in Korea.

Barely had the Korean war concluded in a far from satisfactory armistice that was little more than a stalemate, than the conflict that would claim thousands more lives in the same part of the world drew to its (first round) conclusion. France, doggedly reoccupying Indo-China after the Second World War, flew in the face of Vietnamese nationalism and created a power struggle that was eventually settled by force of arms.

The increasing strength and determination of the Viet Minh to throw off colonial shackles for good led to a gradual escalation of combat at the end of the 1940s and into the early 1950s. A war fought largely by obsolescent aircraft in support of some very dubious military ventures on the ground, Indo-China provided invaluable lessons for the future conduct of ground and air operations against a tenacious foe. Unfortunately for France, the lessons came too late.

Throughout the campaign, the French naval and air force elements were hampered by lack of modern equipment, particularly bombers with a substantial load-carrying capability. American material assistance in the form of US crews flying their own B-29s against the Viet Minh was refused; instead the US loaned two bomber types, the B-26 Invader and the PB4Y-2 Privateer for Air Force and Navy use respectively. Both ably supported the army offensive but neither could do more than shore up a rapidly deteriorating situation.

The first Invaders arrived at Tan Son Nhut air base near Saigon in November 1950 and the first unit to be equipped, GB I/19 Gascogne, was formed on 1 January 1951. These aircraft, a mix of B-26B and C models, were quickly and frequently called upon. The precedent for the later debacle at Dien Bien Phu was at Nghia Lo. Set in a basin surrounded by mountains, the Viet Minh forces under the command of the redoubtable General Vo Nguyen Giap were soundly beaten when they attacked the French garrison. Invaders and other types maintained a well co-ordinated series of air strikes against which the Vietnamese had little defence. Between 2 and 15 October 1951 Giap's guerrillas were pounded from the air and finally forced to abandon the planned annihilation of the French outpost.

One lesson the French learned at Nghia Lo was that a beleaguered force can never have enough air support, both in terms of combat aircraft to hit the enemy and transports to bring in supplies. The end of the Korean war released a substantial number of US cargo planes, and more B-26s were shipped to Indo-China to equip a second *Groupe de Bombardement* and to boost the *Armée de l'Air*'s reconnaissance force in the region.

The *Aeronavale*'s contribution to holding the Viet Minh had included the use of US Douglas SBD-5 Dauntlesses operating from the carrier *Dixmude*. These dive bombers in the hands of *Flotille 4F* were, in the spring of 1949, virtually the only aircraft available to support the ground forces. Subsequent US supplies included SB2C-5 Helldivers and F6F-5 Hellcats, both of which saw combat. The Navy's Privateers, operated by *Flotille 8F* (later *28F*) were the only heavy bombers available. Few in number, their contribution was relatively small.

If the French could bring their airpower to bear and catch the Viet Minh off guard, their superiority in firepower invariably inflicted heavy losses. But the Vietnamese were masters of concealment and habitually survived on rations that were little more than

Indo-China and Suez

starvation level to a Westerner – and they never lost an overwhelming superiority in manpower.

Thus the French embarked on the Dien Bien Phu operation on 20 November 1953. For some three months the Viet Minh labored to bring up troops, supplies and guns under constant surveillance and attack by French aircrews. When on 13 March their heavy artillery opened fire, the situation rapidly deteriorated. Airpower was employed around the clock, the Invaders being on station over the approaches to Dien Bien Phu almost on a daily basis. The US supplied another 60 aircraft to help stem the tide and at least enable the base to hold out until relief columns could arrive. GB I/19 converted to B-26s before the end finally arrived, on 7 May. The ceasefire was signed in Geneva on 27 July 1954.

In the meantime, the French aero industry had been planning to re-equip the country's military forces with indigenous weapons,

LEFT: US Douglas SBD-5 Dauntless divebombers operated from US aircraft carriers stationed in the South China Sea. They provided vital air support to the French forces in Indo-China.

particularly aircraft, and in 1952 the first bomber design emerged. Still hampered by a modest defense budget, France made every effort to concentrate production on relatively few first line types. A considerable amount of research was undertaken, but the emphasis was definitely on fighters and small ground attack types.

A bold effort to combine both these roles with that of conventional bombing, was the Sud-Aviation Vautour. With no direct equivalent anywhere else in the world, the Vautour featured a fully swept wing with two underslung SNECMA Atar turbojets and was designed to be a single or dual seater depending on the role. The first of three prototypes flew on 16 October 1952; these night fighter/interceptor variants were followed in July 1957 by the maiden flight of the bomber version designated Vautour IIB. Introducing a glazed nose cone for a bombardier, this variant was equipped to deliver up to 4500 pounds of bombs from a single fuselage bay. Four underwing stations could boost the ordnance load by a further 4000 pounds.

Important in that it was the first type to give crews experience on jet bombers, the Vautour IIB represented a new strength in French military aviation. Anticipating French possession of 'the bomb', the *Armée de l'Air* formed the nucleus of a strategic bomber force around the Vautour, pending the appearance of something more potent

from the ubiquitous Dassault stable.

No sooner had France pulled out of Indo-China than she was faced with conflict much closer to home. In November 1954 civil war broke out in Algeria, leading to eight years of bitterness and bloodshed before independence from France was achieved. To contain the uprising and support her troops in the field, France once again obtained aircraft from the US. The French bomber force drew its strength from a nucleus of B-26 Invaders, 40 of the perennial mediums being supplied by the end of 1954. Others would follow to participate in a long series of sporadic, small-

LEFT: A Consolidated PB4Y-2 Privateer of a Navy patrol squadron flying off the Miami coast in 1948.

BOTTOM LEFT: A Victor tanker escorts two F-111 bombers.

RIGHT: One of the few Western European medium jet designs, the Sud Vautour was an important French type.

BELOW: A Vautour IIN of ECTT 30 at Le Bourget in March 1981.

scale operations which demanded greater use of low-level ground attack type sorties rather than bomber strikes.

Hard on the heels of the Algerian problem came Egypt's nationalization of the Suez Canal, and an obligation by Anglo-French forces to intervene in support of Israel's military operations in the region. The gross over-reaction by Britain against the actions of Colonel Nasser gave military action an impetus of its own, a move supported by France in the belief that a quick victory in Egypt would largely remove the power base from which unrest in Algeria originated. Israel had a high stake in seeing the threat to her security from an increasingly powerful neighbor nullified. While the military threat to Israel from Egypt was real enough (as would become apparent some years later) Nasser's reaction to Suez in 1956 was an immense blow to British pride. That pride was hardly boosted by military success that autumn.

When Operation 'Musketeer' was finally given the go-ahead, the RAF bomber force was tasked with neutralizing the Egyptian Air Force. A massive build-up of squadrons

RIGHT: A Canberra B 2 trails a fuel line from an FR Mk 16 hose drum to refuel a Gloster Javelin. The drum was later fitted to Valiant tankers.

BELOW: New Valiants of No. 232 OCU – the first V-Bomber unit – lined up on the runway at Gaydon, 1956.

on Malta and Cyprus was complete by the time an ultimatum was delivered to Nasser to cease military operations and withdraw his forces ten miles from the canal. The same terms were made known to Israel, whose forces had not then advanced to within the ten mile limit. Israel agreed the terms – but Egypt did not and the Anglo-French invasion was on.

Cyprus then housed a Wing of 62 Canberra B-2s and -6s from seven squadrons, while another 29 Canberras from another four squadrons, and four squadrons of Valiants totaling 24 aircraft, formed a second strike wing on Malta. First to attack were Nos 10 and 12 Squadrons who sent a Canberra strike over Egyptian airfields on the night of 31 October/1 November. Also operating that night were the Valiants on No 148 Sqn. Targets were mainly four airfields in the delta region and eight adjacent to the canal.

Egyptian reaction was at best meager and at worst, non-existent. With the might of three countries ranged against him, Nasser could do little but increase the volume of his rhetoric and bemoan the eventual loss of 260 aircraft, including Il-28 bombers, on the ground. Bombing operations by the RAF continued for two more nights with carrier and land-based strike aircraft flying daylight sorties. Militarily the venture was a walkover; British and French paratroops landed safely, carried out their briefed tasks and were covered by a solid umbrella of friendly airpower. The last men were out of Egypt by 23 December and the bombers had returned home by January 1957.

In the middle of the Suez crisis, Russia

threatened to use her nuclear missile forces if the operations were not terminated. It was a hollow threat but it did serve to highlight the slow build-up of British and French independent nuclear deterrent forces. But even as the Operation 'Musketeer' bombers returned home, the RAF was preparing to test the first British H-bomb 'live' in the Pacific.

Following the first test drop of an A-bomb by a Valiant of No 46 Squadron at Maralinga in southern Australia on 11 October 1956, No 148 Sqn was chosen to carry out the thermonuclear bomb tests. The unit had been the only Valiant squadron to drop bombs in anger during Suez, so the choice was appro-

priate. At the spearhead of a massive support effort, Valiant XD818 took off for a point off Malden Atoll, some 400 miles south of Christmas Island where the Operation 'Grapple' bombers were temporarily based, early on the morning of 15 May 1957.

The awesome detonation of the bomb was followed by another on 31 May and five more until November 1958, thus completing the 'Grapple' series. At last, with each aircraft in the V-force capable of delivering a weapon that in one casing was equal in destructive power to all the bombs dropped by the RAF in World War II, Britain could meet the potential threat from the East.

During the latter half of the twentieth century, the spread of knowledge increased the risk that nations other than the superpowers would obtain the means to manufacture nuclear weapons. By and large this know-how has not resulted in proliferation and the capability to deliver nuclear missiles by aircraft and submarine across continents and oceans has remained in the hands of five countries – the US, USSR, Britain, China and France.

Having exploded its first atomic bomb on 13 February 1960, France went on to build a small but effective 'strategic air command' based around the Mirage IVA, the *Forces Aériennes Stratégique*. Otherwise known as the '*force de dissuasion*', the FAS was formed as a part of an overall nuclear capability, which includes submarine and land-based strategic missiles as well as air-launched tactical nuclear weapons.

Utilizing a delta wing and general design characteristics of the Mirage III series, the Mirage IVA was a two-seater with a much larger airframe than its fighter counterparts. The prototype flew for the first time on 17 June 1959 powered by two Atar 09 B turbojets each offering 13,230 pounds of thrust with afterburning. The aircraft attained a speed of Mach 1.9 early in its flight tests and early production aircraft were configured to carry a single, up to 50-kiloton yield freefall nuclear weapon semi-recessed into the fuselage.

To support the FAS Mirage force, France purchased 12 KC-135 tankers, the first arriving in February 1964; that October the *91e Escadre de Bombardement* was formed at Mont de Marsan. Fifty Mirage IVAs were ordered initially, and this number was subsequently increased to 62.

Before the armistice was signed in Korea, the US flew the prototype of what was arguably its most important heavy bomber type; conceived as the ultimate delivery system in America's cold war arsenal, it became a devastating weapon in both tactical and strategic terms in Vietnam. The bomber was the Boeing B-52 Stratofortress, the biggest of the USAF's 'big sticks', a key element of the defense triumvirate which was completed by ICBMs and atomic submarines. So important did the B-52 program become that it grew to be the one aircraft that for a time, represented the knife-edge choice between man's ability to destroy himself, or to pull back from the brink and allow more sensible counsel to prevail. From the time it entered service in 1955 to the time it flew its first mission in Vietnam on 18 June 1965, the B-52 was the foremost bargaining pawn in superpower politics – had a B-52 strike been launched against the Soviet Union at any time during

that disturbed decade one can only speculate pessimistically on what kind of a world there would be today.

There is no doubt, however, that, given the tense international situation in the 1950s, the B-52 was the bomber the USAF's Strategic Air Command had to have. Design studies began in April 1945 in line with Air Force needs for a future turbojet long-range bomber. Boeing began work as a parallel development of the B-47 and by June 1946 the company was awarded a development contract for an aircraft in the 400 to 500,000 pound class to meet the main requirement of long range.

Gradually the design evolved into a bigger version of the Stratojet, with eight engines and a 35 degree swept wing; on 29 November 1951 the first of two XB-52s was rolled out for

CHAPTER SEVEN

Vietnam and B-52s

ground tests. In the event it was the development YB-52 that flew first, on 15 April 1952. The XB-52 made its maiden flight on 2 October that year.

Similar in conception to the B-47, the new bomber had a wing span of 185 feet and was over 160 feet long. Each of its eight J57 engines was housed in an underslung wing pod and paired with a second powerplant; inflight refueling was also provided. So promising were the performance figures – including a range of some 6000 miles – that the Air Force ordered its first B-52s off the drawing board. Of 13 early production aircraft ordered, only three were completed as B-52As before the improved B model was announced. The B-52A introduced the side-by-side crew seating as against the tandem arrangement in the XB and YB-52s, uprated engines and provision for fuel tanks holding 1000 gallons of fuel under the outer wing panels.

The next models were the B-52B, of which

FAR LEFT: Nosing in under the tail boomer's position, a B-52G prepares to fill up from a KC-135 during Exercise Global Shield in July 1979.

TOP LEFT: French airborne nuclear deterrence is vested in squadrons equipped with the Mirage IV, the largest airframe of the series.

BOTTOM LEFT: The similarity between the Mirage III fighter and the larger bomber is obvious.

RIGHT: A primary weapon of the B-52 is currently SRAM – Short Range Attack Missile – one of which is being launched here.

BELOW: A B-52G heads out on a mission.

BELOW: Cold War warriors trained in unarmed TB-47Bs stationed at McConnell AFB, Kansas.

TOP RIGHT: Impressive in anyone's book, the B-52G is now older than many of its crews.

BELOW RIGHT: Lights on and brake chute streaming, a B-52G lands at Fairford in September 1986.

there were 23, and the RB-52B. There were 27 of these latter 'multi-mission' models, the standard bombing capability being enhanced by a pressurized pod complete with two-man crew who worked on a demanding electronic countermeasures program all but cut off from the rest of the bomber's crew. The pod also had four camera stations.

While the weight of the newer B-52 models had inevitably risen (to 420,000 pounds from the 390,000 pounds of the prototype/preproduction aircraft) the enormous price tag of $29.3 million for each B-52A had dropped to $14.4m apiece for the more numerous B-52Bs, and $7.2m for each of the 35 B-52Cs.

Deliveries of the B-52 to SAC commenced in June 1955, the 93rd HBW at Castle AFB, California, being the first to convert. On 21 May 1956 a B-52B dropped the first US hydrogen bomb over Bikini Atoll in the Pacific, some two months after the first C model made its maiden flight. Three weeks after Bikini, SAC took delivery of the B-52C and, to illustrate how urgent the build-up of the B-52 force was, by Christmas the D model had also entered service. The D model was the first to be built by both Seattle and Wichita plants and was followed by the B-52E with similar split production, then the F model, which saw the end of Seattle's part in the program, the subsequent B-52G being built only at Wichita.

Externally the B-52G brought the most noticeable change; the height of the fin and rudder was reduced and ailerons were dispensed with, but inside, the aircraft was almost entirely new. Further revisions — to increase payload, lower gross weight and boost the range — were incorporated into the

final production model, the B-52H. Production of the G model reached a peak with 193 examples, the Wichita line completing a further 102 H models before B-52 output was terminated after a grand total of 744 aircraft had been built. A B-52H cost the US taxpayer just $5.4m, although the higher volume G model had, on some contracts, fallen as low as $3.4m.

By the time the last B-52H was delivered to the USAF on 26 October 1962, the type had seen very widespread service; no fewer than 69 Wings had used the B-52 at various periods and in a variety of roles. Primarily the Stratofortress served in its designed role as a high level bomber, equally capable of delivering nuclear or conventional bombs on targets up to 5000 miles from its home bases. And its weaponry was not restricted to the somewhat antiquated 'gravity' drop variety with all its attendant risk to aircraft and crew when the target had to be overflown. Much money and research time went into providing the SAC heavy bomber force with true stand-off capability and although there were a number of costly failures, such systems were to mature after the B-52 had proved to be a devastating weapon in combat — with iron bombs.

In total, four bombers saw action over North and South Vietnam, the B-52 being joined by the B-57 and B-66 in the early stages, with the F-111 doing its bit a little later. In a war dominated by fighter-bomber operations to support troops in the field and, in the case of North Vietnam, to knock out the enemy's industrial base, all US bombers were employed in their designated roles,

TOP: Douglas RB-66Bs at Takhli, Thailand on Christmas Day, 1968.

ABOVE: Characteristic smoky engine start for a 3rd Bomb Wing B-57 at Tan Son Nhut, Vietnam in 1965.

ABOVE RIGHT: An F-111's purposeful silhouette over Upper Heyford in April 1986.

RIGHT: A terrain-hugging practice bomb run for the B-1B.

short life span of some five years. It was fortunate that the 3rd BG which had received the type in 1957, still had operational aircraft in Japan in 1964, the year that the situation in South Vietnam deteriorated to the point where US aircraft began overtly flying combat missions. For ten years the B-57 would give valuable service in Southeast Asia.

The B-57B was followed by the C model dual control trainer, the specialized intruder B-57G, and the B-57E target tug. For high altitude reconnaissance there was the RB-57D and the General Dynamics RB-57F. The entire series was subject to further adaptation for special roles, but the attack mission was largely handled by the B and G models flown by the 3rd Bomb Wing.

More complex (and costly) changes were required by the USAF to adapt the Navy Douglas A3D Skywarrior to the tactical light bombing and reconnaissance role. The first aircraft flew on 28 June 1954 as an RB-66A — an indication of how important ECM and photo surveillance had become by this time. While the B-66 was not alone in flying most of its operational sorties in roles other than bombing, it was utilized more on recon work than other types: only 72 aircraft were built as bombers, and 13 of these were converted to EB-66B configuration. In Vietnam, the B-66 was to serve as a 'pathfinder' for fighter bomber strikes, as an ECM platform and a general reconnaissance type, the hauling of high explosives having long been the province of smaller, more agile aircraft. The size of the B-66 meant that its multiple crew stations could be better utilized by electronic equipment operators and these crews gave a valuable service in the vital airborne early warning role.

As the Southeast Asian war gained momentum, a group of men gathered at Forth Worth, Texas, and breathed a collective sigh of relief as a new aircraft lifted off the runway on 21 December 1964. The highly controversial General Dynamics F-111A had finally flown. An attempt to embody the widely differing requirements of the US Navy and Air Force (not to mention the RAF, which, denied the promising TSR-2, was obliged to fill the gap with American aircraft), the TFX program would have replaced the F-4 Phantom and F-105 Thunderchief respectively in the US services. In the event, the USAF was the sole recipient of the variable geometry F-111, when the Navy requirement was canceled.

Despite its designation, the F-111 was never thought of as a fighter. Instead it offered a second-to-none capability as a strike bomber, particularly at low level. Delivery to the first of four Wings that would operate the F-111 started in October 1967 and in March 1968 six aircraft were assigned to

with only the B-66 Destroyer undertaking a supportive role as an ECM platform. The rules of engagement created by the US to hamper rather than contain the war in the North, saw strategic targets attacked by tactical aircraft; not until the end of the US involvement were the B-52s unleashed against strategic targets — with predictably devastating results.

As mentioned previously, the US had an urgent need to replace the B-26 Invader with a more modern aircraft able to carry out a similar mission, particularly that of night intruder. Opening a production line and initiating 'Americanization' of the British Canberra was an astute move which saved both time and development costs, and in consequence the first B-57 made its maiden flight on 20 July 1953.

Similar to the Canberra B.2, the B-57A was the forerunner of the major US production version, the B-57B. In this the Martin company produced a version with no British equivalent and with General Dynamics, this firm would go on to build new models which had to be near the absolute limit of adaptation of a basic airframe.

With its use restricted to three bomb groups, the 461st, 345th and 38th, in the US and Europe, the B-57B had a comparatively the 428th TFS for trials in Vietnam. Under combat conditions, the performance of the F-111 was a disappointment, leading to the belief that the aircraft could not fulfill its role. This turned out to be quite untrue, as was proven four years later when two squadrons of the 474th TFW went back to the war zone and proceeded to carry out some of the most demanding and dangerous combat missions of the entire war with outstanding success. The F-111 was viewed as a partial replacement for ageing B-52s in the SAC fleet, as well as another bomber which many believed was prematurely retired. This was the dramatic and radical Convair B-58 Hustler, the first supersonic bomber to enter USAF service.

Employing a delta wing spanning almost 57 feet, the B-58 was powered by four J79 turbojets of 15,600 pounds each, giving it a maximum speed of 1385 mph at 40,000 feet and a service ceiling of more than 63,000 feet. The fuselage embodied area rule aerodynamic principles and to save weight, no ordnance was carried internally. Instead, the B-58 was provided with a huge underslung pod containing fuel which was used en route to the target, and a nuclear weapon. Once the mission had been completed, the pod was jettisoned for a high speed dash home.

The B-58 first flew on 11 November 1956; 30 test aircraft were followed by 86 B-58A models, the first Hustler Wing being the

43rd, activated in March 1960. The 305th became the second B-58 unit and these two Wings operated the Hustler from Carswell and Bunker Hill Air Force Bases until the B-58 was withdrawn in 1970. Among the reasons for this move was the average unit cost of one B-58 – a cool $33.5 m, and an accusation that the aircraft had a poor safety record. Nevertheless, the B-58 was a technical masterpiece and it explored many areas of military flying at the operational as well as test level, that were not duplicated by any other type of comparable size for some years.

Vietnam sorties for the B-57 Canberra were concurrent with the start of combat operations by US (rather than South Vietnamese) crews against Viet Cong guerrillas infiltrating southern regions of the country. The first such mission was flown on 19 February 1965 and took the bombers into North Vietnam to attack an enemy staging area. At that time North Vietnam had yet to build up what became a formidable air defense net, and some successful operations were mounted by aircraft that did not have the sophisticated self-protection and offensive weapons that were to arrive later in the 'Rolling Thunder' bombing campaign.

It was, however, the B-52s which were to make the biggest impact – explosively and psychologically – on the enemy. Under the generic designation 'Arc Light', SAC sent its strategic bombers on tactical sorties, to carpet-bomb vast tracts of jungle which were suspected of harboring Viet Cong or North Vietnamese concentrations of troops and/or supplies. It became apparent that in some cases, the B-52s were merely destroying trees, but unlike any other form of air attack, the rain of bombs was totally unexpected. Even quick reaction strikes by fast jets failed at times to nail the enemy, who could quickly melt away at the slightest hint of air attack, but 'Arc Light' strikes were loathed and feared.

They were carried out by SAC bomb wings which rotated into Andersen AB on the island of Guam for an average of four months' combat duty. Guam is some 2600 miles from the southern regions of Vietnam and each strike, composed of multiple three-plane 'cells' of B-52s supported by tankers, involved a mission time of about 12 hours. Initially the 7th, 320th, 454th, 22nd, 91st and 306th Wings rotated to Guam and in the first year these units dropped more than 100,000 tons of bombs in more than 3800 sorties.

'Arc Light' strikes were gradually increased in scope to stabilize at about 350-400 sorties per month; an increase in the number of raids on targets in Laos escalated in parallel with the intensity of the fighting in Vietnam, although these were far smaller in

terms of B-52 sorties. Not that a vast number of sorties were needed: each B-52D and F could carry up to 60,000 pounds of bombs internally and on two underwing racks. That weight of bombs, generally in 500 pound and 750 pound sizes, could be delivered by each B-52 with remarkable accuracy, so much so that Gen William Westmoreland, head of Military Assistance Command, Vietnam (MACV), constantly requested an increase in

The expensive B-58 Hustler had a relatively short career. It was retired in 1969-70 having made a significant contribution to SAC as a deterrent force.

TOP LEFT: The important secondary duty of target towing was carried out by the B-57E. This one has the distinctive red and silver markings of the 3rd TTS from George AFB.

LEFT: A B-66B flips inverted while testing toss bombing at Edwards AFB in November 1957.

sortie rate to aid the ground forces. Questioned as to exactly what the big bombers – BUFFs or Big Ugly Flying Fellows to their crews – hit on their high altitude runs, Westmoreland and other high ranking officers tended to emphasise the psychological impact of the bomb carpets.

SAC however had to marshal its strategic bomber force carefully; with the B-58 phasing out and the F-111 just entering service, loss of a significant number of B-52s, to whatever cause, could adversely effect the command's primary mission, which was the defense of the United States. In the event, attrition rate in the B-52 force in combat over Vietnam was remarkably light in this 'iron bomb war' which hardly anyone in SAC had planned for.

In April 1967 three B-52s landed at U-Tapao in Thailand, heralding the use of that base for heavy bomber operations until the end of the war. Basing B-52s at U-Tapao was a great relief to the crews, who were consequently far nearer their targets than their colleagues on Guam. On flights of only three to five hours' duration there was no need for air refueling.

Until September 1967, the B-52s faced few hazards, but that month the first SAMs were

fired against the big bombers. Efficient deception equipment aboard the aircraft, plus evasive action, saw the missiles explode harmlessly on this occasion. The enemy was henceforth to fire off a prodigious number of SA-2s at B-52s, with only a tiny percentage managing to bring a bomber down. Throughout this phase of the war, leading to the 1968 Tet Offensive, reports from captured enemy troops verified the fear engendered by B-52 strikes. And by 1968 Westmoreland had his required sortie rate of 1800 a month. Reaching a peak in March, B-52s operated continually in support of the defenders of Khe Sahn, flying 1852 sorties before the seemingly 'impossible' enemy offensive throughout South Vietnam wrecked US plans to pursue the war to a satisfactory conclusion. President Lyndon Johnson restricted bombing in two phases and by the autumn, it was halted completely.

As events were to prove, the war was not over. In between the end of 'Rolling Thunder' and the start of 'Linebacker' in 1972, B-52s remained on standby, missions being flown at a reduced rate to targets in Cambodia. By 1970, both Guam and Kadena on Okinawa were flying a very low level of sorties, the main B-52 activity being centered on

U-Tapao. It was in many ways, the calm before the storm.

When the NVA invaded South Vietnam in the spring of 1972, the US at last had many clearly defined military targets to attack; for some eight months the South Vietnamese fought their Northern countrymen largely without US help on the ground. Under the policy of 'Vietnamization' American troop withdrawals left a national army that was strong in some areas, but disastrously weak in others. In the air, American fighters and bombers remained to give able support to their Allies. The peace talks, stalled since 1969, continued to await a military solution.

As autumn approached, US air forces were flying an increasing number of support sorties — this time with better tactics and weapons. Plans were made to use the B-52s against Hanoi, if a satisfactory peace could

BELOW: An H model Buff enters a little weather on a training flight.

BELOW RIGHT: A B-58 Hustler crew keeping an eye on the tanker boom during a 1968 sortie.

not otherwise be concluded. President Richard Nixon had halted all bombing above the 20th parallel in October but by December, nothing had been achieved at the negotiating table. It was decided to use the B-52s in an intensive night bombing campaign against the most important targets in the North. 'Linebacker II' began on 18 December with three wings of B-52Ds and one with 'G' models sharing the attack. At high altitudes —

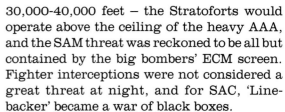

30,000-40,000 feet — the Stratoforts would operate above the ceiling of the heavy AAA, and the SAM threat was reckoned to be all but contained by the big bombers' ECM screen. Fighter interceptions were not considered a great threat at night, and for SAC, 'Linebacker' became a war of black boxes.

Predictions proved to be true enough; for eleven days the B-52s bombed out the industrial heartland of North Vietnam to such an extent that many people believed they had achieved more in a few weeks than 'Rolling Thunder' had in four years. More than 20,000 tons of high explosive was dropped with extreme accuracy in 729 B-52 sorties until 30 December when the North indicated a desire to resume peace talks. So effective were the B-52 raids deemed to be that as long as the US was prepared to fly in support of ground operations, the South Vietnamese wanted such assistance and it was not until 15 August 1973 that the last bomb was dropped by a B-52 in Southeast Asia.

In an age that saw the rise of the fighter bomber armed with a comprehensive array of self-protection and detection devices plus a substantial offensive load, the B-52 proved in Vietnam that there was still a place for the 'big stick' despite the deployment of SAMs (albeit in a rather primitive form) against them. The 'Linebacker' losses of 15 bombers, slightly over 2% of the force engaged, was militarily acceptable. Whether such a campaign could ever be conducted again was, however, doubtful even as America stood down its forces. Half a decade on, it was seen that the rapid pace of missile technology had made the 'Linebacker' raids truly the end of the era of the heavy bomber attacking targets with gravity bombs.

The world did not stop development of bomber aircraft. All the time strategic elements were supported by the US and Soviet Union, new equipment was needed to replace the old. In the US the extreme longevity of the B-52 fleet, many examples of which were older than the crews who flew them, gave good return on the taxpayers' dollar, but by the late 1960s there was an urgent need for a replacement. It was important to initiate a new long-range bomber program and North American Rockwell responded with the variable geometry B-1.

Under the acronym AMSA – Advanced Manned Strategic Aircraft – the USAF selected the B-1 in 1970. Designed to be equally at home in high and low altitude attack modes, using a variety of stand-off and conventional weapons, the B-1 has had a chequered career. The first prototype made its maiden flight on 23 December 1974 with three others following in 1976 and 1979. But in 1977 the project was canceled by President Jimmy Carter, mainly for budgetary reasons.

Research and development flying continued however until April 1981 when the last (it was presumed) flight was made by the fourth aircraft. The project remained dormant until it was resurrected to meet the USAF's LRCA – Long Range Combat Aircraft – requirements. The B-1 was to be the air element of the US strategic nuclear deterrent, otherwise composed of land-based and submarine-borne missiles. The necessary financial incentive was provided by the Reagan Administration in October 1981. An order for 100 B-1s was placed and Rockwell began a series of modifications to the test aircraft to tailor them to a dual role. The second 'first flights' were made in March 1983 and July 1984. Now the B-1's primary mission was that of cruise missile carrier, launching its load outside the range of enemy defenses. Secondary was the ability to carry conventional ordnance, and missiles. In line with current state-of-the-art defense technology, the B-1 had its radar signature reduced significantly.

The service model, the B-1B, made its maiden flight on 18 October 1984. A year later the 96th Bomb Wing became the first to receive the type and by the time production was completed in 1988 the USAF had accepted enough B-1Bs to equip four Wings. These aircraft are intended to remain in service throughout the 1990s.

How many B-2s will be available to support any serious downturn in US relations with other nations of the world remains a matter of conjecture. The enormous cost of the so-called 'Stealth' bomber, plus the Lockheed F-117 fighter which employs similar highly advanced technology, within the ramifications of a decrease in international tension in Eastern Europe, might eventually be seen to be money poorly invested in aircraft that will never be deployed 'in anger' and will never be used to their full potential.

It was in 1981 that the USAF selected Northrop to initiate development of an ATB – Advanced Technology Bomber – utilizing materials and techniques that would make the aircraft a very tough target for enemy defenses. Encompassing the airframe into a flying wing, a configuration that Northrop had explored extensively in the 1950s, the B-2 flew for the first time on 17 July 1989.

A highly unconventional design, the B-2 is powered by four GE F118 non-afterburning turbofans buried in the wing root area adjacent to the cockpit. A crew of two or three can be carried, depending on mission. Dimen-

CHAPTER EIGHT

Modern Bombers

sions of the B-2 include a wingspan of approximately 172 feet, a length of 69 feet and a height of 17 feet. A bomb load, less than that of the B-1, is accommodated in an internal weapons bay.

Under a program costing $42.5 bn, the USAF has ordered 132 B-2s for service into the twenty-first century, although defense budget revisions could see some modification of this figure. At present the B-2 is envisaged as part of a bomber inventory currently composed of 97 B-1Bs, 261 B-52G/Hs and 61 FB-111As.

On the Soviet scene an updating of the bomber force led, in the mid-1980s, to the development of a long range Tupolev design known by the NATO codename 'Blackjack'. About 20 per cent larger than the B-1 it was publicly announced in 1988, by which time the first unit had been formed. Designated Tu-160, the Blackjack does not, unlike the B-1, employ any obvious stealth technology but is a VG aircraft. A 'guesstimated' speed of

OPPOSITE: The sleek snout of the B-1B low over mountainous country. SAC's 97-strong fleet is dispersed on four bases throughout the US. Current plans forsee B-1s serving well into the 21st century.

MAIN PICTURE: When the B-1 program was restarted, Rockwell made up time as fast as possible, enabling the first B model to fly on 23 March 1983.

RIGHT: With wings fully swept, the B-1B is subsonic at low level but supersonic at altitude.

The newest shapes in US skies are the stealth fighter and bomber. The latter, the Northrop B-2 completed initial flight tests on 23 September 1989. These included positioning, but not actual fuel transfer, from a KC-10 Extender.

LEFT: Edwards AFB, July 1989. A new aircraft takes off on its first flight and the USAF steps into a new era. A sortie to 10,000 feet began a series of intensive flight tests.

BELOW: The B-2 is perhaps the ultimate development of the flying wing, a Northrop speciality.

RIGHT: With rubber mats protecting the radar wave-absorbent skin, the B-2 line at Palmdale represents a bill of $1,500,000,00 for three aircraft.

Mach 2.3 has been announced by the US Defense Department.

The Blackjack, of which 100 are believed to have been ordered for the VVS, joins an inventory currently comprising 350 Tu-26 Backfires, some 270 Tu-16s, and 170 Tu-142 Bears. In addition there are 120 medium-range Tu-22 Blinders. In the slightly un-realistic but convenient grouping of Eastern and Western air arms, one could not, in con-sideration of bomber forces, overlook Red China. Basically a defensive force, the PLAAF (Air Force) maintains numerous examples (about 120) of the Xian H-6 which is a Chinese copy of the Tu-16. As important to the Chinese aero industry as the pirated B-29 was to the Soviets, the Xian H-6 was a simi-larly unauthorized duplication made in 1967.

China also has a medium bomber force composed entirely of obsolete Harbin H-5s (Il-28s) numbering about 500 examples. A new long-range bomber is rumored to be under development in the People's Republic, and this will eventually join the nuclear and cruise missile-capable Xian H-6 force. The Tu-16 was itself supplied to Indonesia before that country broke its Soviet links in the later 1960s. The 24 bombers came complete with Kennel cruise missiles, but few are believed to be operational now.

At the start of the 1990s, the easing of superpower tension would appear to reduce still further the need for intercontinental attack weapons, particularly long range bombers. Ongoing and ever-deepening defense cuts linked to further ratification of arms reduction treaties between East and West could indeed spell the eventual end of any aircraft of this type.

Nevertheless, numerous bombs have been dropped from aircraft ever since the end of the Vietnam war and nations still resort to this kind of retaliation from time to time. The Israeli air force, for example, has often been placed on alert in response to hostile acts by her neighbors. Even the superpowers are not beyond a high explosive response to per-ceived aggression – witness the US air strikes in Lebanon and the controversial 'Eldorado Canyon' USAF attack on Colonel Gadaffi's Libya in April 1986. Politically such provocative acts of national will appear in-creasingly risky, out of all proportion to re-sults achieved militarily – but that is not to say that the day of the bomber is past. In the early 1980s Britain contemplated replacing the last of the 'V' bombers with a smaller RAF force composed entirely of fighters . . . but after the Argentine invasion of the Falkland Islands in 1982, the British government had cause to rethink their decision. The bombing

ABOVE: The infamous Backfire gave the West a big headache ages before it was revealed to be the potent Mach 2 Tu-26. The ache remains!

TOP RIGHT: A Tu-16 Badger caught on a recon sortie over the UK.

RIGHT: Heavy cannon armament was fitted to the Badger-A, as seen on this one operating northwest of Japan.

RIGHT: The US DOD put out this impression before details of the Tu-160 Blackjack were known.

BELOW: In marked contrast, a Vulcan B 2 of No 50 Squadron RAF represents a bomber era that is rapidly passing.

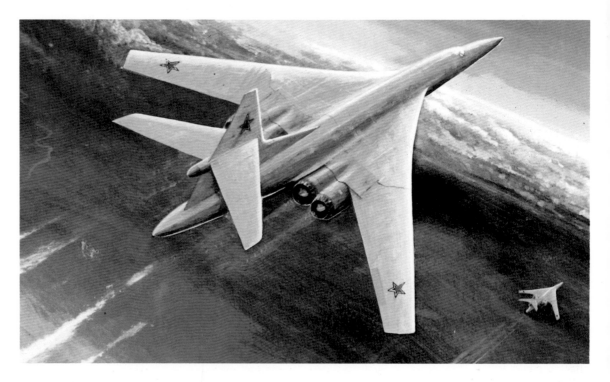

of the runway at Port Stanley proved the Vulcans' worth and probably won a small reprieve for long-range bombers everywhere.

It has been said that just as the appearance of a gunboat on the horizon in the last century signaled the serious displeasure of one of the great powers, so today the size of the aircraft deployed in a given situation can be used as a yardstick of national intent. Given the fact that many countries are still prepared to back up the invective of their politicians with military might, it seems likely that bomber aircraft will be around in some form for some years to come.

INDEX

ACKNOWLEDGMENTS

The Publishers would like to thank Design-23, Moira Dykes for picture research and Ron Watson for the index. They would also like to thank the following agencies and institutions for the use of photographs on the pages noted below:

Austin J Brown, Aviation Picture Library: pages 2, 11 below, 20 top, 28, 51 below, 55 top, 59 below, 61 below, 63 top, 74-75
Bison Picture Library: pages 37 below, 58 top
Hulton-Deutsch Collection: pages 20 below, 44, 52
Robert Hunt Picture Library: page 8 below
Imperial War Museum, London: pages 8 top, 9
MARS/Boeing Aircraft Company, USA: pages 5, 6, 12, 17, 22 below, 40 top, 66-67/British Aerospace: page 78 below/ECP Armees: page 51 top/Flight Refuelling: pages 52-53/Martin Aircraft Company: page 23 below/MOD-RAF, London: pages 1 right, 24 top, 29, 30 top, 46 below, 54 top, 61 top/MOD-RN: pages 38-39/Northrop Corp: page 75 top/Rockwell International, USA: pages 1 left, 16 below, 68/Vickers Ltd: pages 26-27
Novosti Press Agency: page 35 below
Photo Press: pages 18 below, 30 below, 54 below
Rockwell International, USA: pages 70-71
Jerry Scutts: pages 2-3, 10, 14-15, 16 top, 18 top, 22 top, 23 top, 25, 31 top, 36, 42-43, 50 both
The Research House: pages 4, 31 below, 34, 45, 46 top, 55 below, 62 both, 65/Boeing: page 19/Dassault-Breguet: page 53 below/DOD: pages 40 below, 72-73, 76, 78 top/NASM: page 60/Vickers: page 26 top
Topham Picture Source: pages 15 top, 23 centre, 24 below
USAF: pages 11 top, 14 both, 59 top/MARS: pages 47 below, 56, 64 below, 67, 71/TRH: pages 1 below, 42 top, 47 top, 63 below, 74 top
US Navy: pages 35 top, 37 top, 77 top/MARS: page 77 below/TRH: pages 32, 48